STONE CIRCLE STORIES:
CULTURE AND FOLKTALES

TALL TALE STORIES

BY
VIRGINIA
LOH-HAGAN

People have been telling stories since the beginning of time. This series focuses on stories found across cultures. You may have heard these stories from your parents or grandparents. Or you may have told one yourself around a campfire. Stories explain the world around us. They inspire. They motivate. They even scare! We tell stories to share our history.

45th Parallel Press

Published in the United States of America by Cherry Lake Publishing
Ann Arbor, Michigan
www.cherrylakepublishing.com

Reading Adviser: Marla Conn MS, Ed., Literacy specialist, Read-Ability, Inc.
Book Designer: Jen Wahi

Photo Credits: ©helenos/Shutterstock.com, 5; ©alexblacksea/Shutterstock.com, 7; ©Joseph Sohm/Shutterstock.com, 8; ©Nina Buday/Shutterstock.com, 11; ©Jannarong/Shutterstock.com, 13; ©Seita/Shutterstock.com, 14; ©Everett Historical/Shutterstock.com, 17; ©Georgios Kollidas/Shutterstock.com, 19; ©Ron and Joe/Shutterstock.com, 21; ©Digital Storn/Shutterstock.com, 23; ©Zmaj88/Shutterstock.com, 25; ©Esteban De Armas/Shutterstock.com, 27; ©DrimaFilm/Shutterstock.com, 28; ©Kostyantyn Ivanyshen/Shutterstock.com, cover and interior; Various grunge/texture patterns throughout courtesy of Shutterstock.com

45th Parallel Press is an imprint of Cherry Lake Publishing.

Library of Congress Cataloging-in-Publication Data

Names: Loh-Hagan, Virginia, author.
Title: Tall tale stories / by Virginia Loh-Hagan.
Description: [Ann Arbor : Cherry Lake Publishing, 2019] | Series: Stone circle stories. Culture and folktales | Includes bibliographical references and index.
Identifiers: LCCN 2018035170| ISBN 9781534143463 (hardcover) | ISBN 9781534140028 (pbk.) | ISBN 9781534141223 (pdf) | ISBN 9781534142428 (hosted ebook)
Subjects: | CYAC: Tall tales. | Folklore.
Classification: LCC PZ8.1.L936 Tal 2019 | DDC [398.2]--dc23
LC record available at https://lccn.loc.gov/2018035170

Printed in the United States of America
Corporate Graphics

ABOUT THE AUTHOR:

Dr. Virginia Loh-Hagan is an author, university professor, and former classroom teacher. She likes all things tall, like giraffes and her husband. She lives in San Diego with her very tall husband and very naughty dogs. To learn more about her, visit www.virginialoh.com.

ABOUT THE AUTHOR 2

INTRODUCTION:
TALL TALE STORIES 4

CHAPTER 1:
PAUL BUNYON
AND BABE THE BLUE OX 6

CHAPTER 2:
CALAMITY JANE 12

CHAPTER 3:
JOHN HENRY 18

CHAPTER 4:
CAPTAIN STORMALONG 24

CHALLENGE: WRITE YOUR OWN TALE 30
CONSIDER THIS! 31
LEARN MORE! 31
GLOSSARY 32
INDEX 32

TABLE OF CONTENTS

TALL TALE STORIES

What are tall tales?

Have you ever **bragged**? Bragging is showing off. People show off their skills. They show off their things. They want others to be impressed. They make their lives seem more exciting.

Tall tales are special stories. They're told as if they're true. But, they're not. They **exaggerate** real facts or events. Exaggerate means to make things seem bigger than they are. Tall tales are realistic stories with unbelievable parts. Some tall tales are based on real people. But, the heroes are taller. They're smarter. They're stronger. They're better than everyone else.

Tall tales combine fact and fiction.

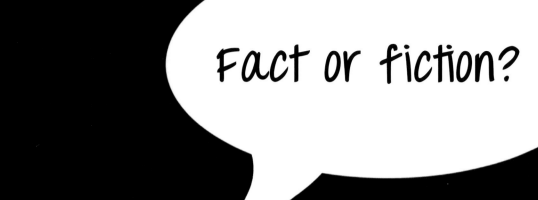

CHAPTER 1

PAUL BUNYAN
AND BABE THE BLUE OX

How big was Paul Bunyan?
How did he find Babe?
What did he and Babe do?

Paul Bunyan was the world's largest baby. Normally, parents carry their babies home from the hospital. But Bunyan was too big. Five giant storks had to carry him.

Normal babies sleep in cribs. But Bunyan was too big. He slept in a wagon. Horses pulled the wagon. His father drove the wagon from one state to another. This was how Bunyan was rocked to sleep.

Babies cry a lot. But Bunyan's cries weren't normal. They were really loud. His cry scared fish out of rivers. It made animals go deaf. Frogs wore earmuffs to block out the sound.

Bunyan has been called the Thor or Hercules of American folk stories.

Some say I'm the original hipster.

Bunyan kept getting bigger. He slept in a big boat. He floated in the ocean. He moved when he slept. This caused big sea storms.

Bunyan was hungry a lot. His stomach rumbled. This caused the earth to shake. Bunyan ate 10 barrels of oatmeal every 2 hours. He drank milk from 2 dozen cows every morning and night.

It was so cold, the snow turned blue.
The blue snow stained Babe.

He grew to be a big man. One day, he walked in the woods. He found a baby blue ox. He took care of the ox. The ox was named Babe the Blue Ox. Babe also grew. He became a giant ox. Bunyan and Babe were super strong.

Bunyan became a **lumberjack**. Lumberjacks cut down trees. They turn trees into logs.

There was a problem. Lumberjacks found a huge log jam by the river. They were piled high. They blocked the river. Only Bunyan and Babe could help. Bunyan put Babe in front of the logs. He shot at Babe. Babe thought the bullet was a fly. He moved his tail back and forth. This moved the logs.

Bunyan created many natural places. His and Babe's footprints made lakes in Minnesota. Bunyan dragged his ax on the ground. This made the Grand Canyon. Babe died of old age. Bunyan was sad. He cried. His tears became the Missouri River.

In some tall tales, Bunyan had a giant wife and giant children.

CHAPTER 2

CALAMITY JANE

Who is Martha Jane Cannary?
How did she become known as "Calamity Jane"?

Imagine having criminals as parents. Imagine being an **orphan** at age 12. Orphans are children whose parents died. **Calamity** Jane's life was a mess. Calamity means disaster.

Jane's real name was Martha Jane Cannary. She was a star of the American Wild West. She did things women didn't do. She did men's jobs. She wore men's clothes. She acted like a man. She rode horses. She shot guns. She was tough and rough. She moved to Deadwood, South Dakota. This town was known for murders and crimes.

Maybe that's why they called it Deadwood?

Calamity Jane served as a scout.
She wore an army uniform.

Jane bragged. She said she was a daring horse rider. She said she was the best shooter. She fought battles against Native Americans. That's how she earned her name. She was in Wyoming. Native Americans attacked her group. They shot her captain. Jane lifted him onto her horse. She brought him safely back. The captain said, "I name

Calamity Jane performed in Wild West shows.

you Calamity Jane, the **heroine** of the **plains**." Heroines are female heroes. Plains are flat lands.

She swam in rivers to deliver messages. She also delivered mail. She rode over rough land. She had a bad temper. Once, she went to a play. She didn't like it. She spit in the actor's eye.

A Native American war party attacked a **stagecoach**. Stagecoaches are carriages. They're pulled by horses.

FAST-FORWARD TO MODERN TIMES

Chuck Norris is a famous actor. He's famous for doing martial arts. He makes action movies and TV shows. He's known as a "tough guy." There are many tall tales about him. These stories exaggerate his toughness. They exaggerate his manliness. Chuck Norris stories are spread around the world. There are tales about how he uses roundhouse kicks to solve problems. There are tales about his body hair. A popular tall tale is about Norris and Mount Rushmore. Mount Rushmore is a national memorial. It's in South Dakota. It's a mountain. It has 4 U.S. presidents carved in it. People say that Norris was going to be added to Mount Rushmore. But the rock wasn't tough enough for his beard.

The stagecoach driver was hit. The horses ran away with the stagecoach. Jane chased it. She jumped on. She took control of the reins. Reins are ropes that control horses. Jane drove the stagecoach back to Deadwood. She saved 6 passengers and the stagecoach driver.

Many people in Deadwood got smallpox. Smallpox is a deadly sickness. Jane helped. She nursed people back to health.

Jane died in 1903. She had a big funeral. Funerals are events that honor people's death. Jane's funeral was Deadwood's largest for a woman.

Calamity Jane was also called "the White Devil of the Yellowstone."

CHAPTER 3

JOHN HENRY

What was John Henry's job?
How did he beat the machine?
How did he die?

John Henry was an African American. He weighed 44 pounds (20 kilograms) at birth. He was born with a hammer in his hand. He started working after his first meal. He grew to be over 8 feet (2.4 meters) tall.

He worked for a railroad company. He was the strongest worker. He was the best worker. No one was better than him. Henry was a "steel-driving man." His job was to swing his hammer. He hammered steel spikes into rocks. The spikes were thick. Henry made holes.

John Henry was born a slave.
He was freed after the Civil War.

Bombs were put into the holes. They blasted the rock.
This was how railroad tunnels were made.

CROSS-CULTURAL CONNECTION

"Manly Man" is a tall tale from northern Nigeria. It's told by the Hausa people. Hausa people are a group of people who live in different parts of West Africa. Manly Man was a very strong man. He did everything better than other men. He cut twice as much wood. He hunted twice as much food. He bragged about how strong he was. His wife warned him that someone stronger would come along. She went to get water from a well. A woman came to help. She asked her strong baby to get the water. The baby's father was also called Manly Man. The wife told her husband. Her husband was upset. He wanted to be the manliest of all men. He went to the well. He saw the strong baby. He asked to meet his father. He wanted to show him who the real Manly Man was. He met a huge giant who ate elephants. He got scared. He ran home. He never called himself Manly Man again.

There was a big mountain. Workers worked over 12 hours a day. They did dangerous work. They were building a tunnel. They risked their lives. They worked for years.

The railroad company wanted to use a new machine. It was a special drill. It was powered by steam. The railroad company said the machine was better than Henry. They said it worked faster. They said it worked better.

The workers were worried. They didn't like the machine. They thought they'd lose their jobs. Henry said, "Before

Henry's hammer was heavy. It weighed over 20 pounds (9 kg).

I'll let your steam drill beat me down, I'll die with my hammer in my hand."

Henry raced the machine. He used 2 heavy hammers. He had one in each hand. He hammered. He drilled. He worked without stopping. He didn't quit.

At the end of the day, Henry won. He beat the machine. He made more holes. But then, he fell. He hit the ground. He was tired. He was stressed. He died. He was buried with his hammer in his hand.

Some people think Henry's face is carved in the tunnel rock. They say they can hear his hammers hitting the rock. Henry is a symbol of African American power. He represents the human spirit.

There's a famous song about John Henry.

CHAPTER 4

CAPTAIN STORMALONG

What is "The Courser"?
How is Stormalong strong?
How did Stormalong die?

Captain Alfred Bulltop Stormalong was a giant. At birth, he was 18 feet (5.5 m) tall. He was **beached** as a baby. Beached means stuck on a beach. Stormalong ate a lot. He ate 6 sharks for breakfast. At age 12, he ran away. He worked on a ship.

Stormalong was from Massachusetts.

He grew to be over 30 feet (9 m) tall. He became the captain of a ship. His ship was called *The Courser*. It was really wide. It was really deep. It could only be in deep water. Its **masts** went up to the sky. Masts are tall posts on ships. They hold sails. The masts had to be moved to avoid hitting the sun and moon.

Stormalong steered *The Courser*. He was the only man strong enough to do it. He kept the ship from hitting islands. He used all his power.

He fought a kraken. A kraken was a big sea monster. Stormalong hunted the kraken. The kraken escaped from him many times. This upset Stormalong. Once, he was mad enough to quit sailing. He became a farmer. But he couldn't stay away. He returned to the sea. He hunted the kraken again. He finally trapped it. He led it to a **whirlpool**. Whirlpools are strong spinning water. They suck things in.

There are several tall tales about Stormalong's death.

This is one story. Stormalong saw a boat on fire. He dumped water on it. The boat's captain was mad. He wanted to race Stormalong. They raced around the world. Stormalong won. But he used all his power. He died.

Sailors rode horses to get from one end of the ship to the other.

This is another story. Stormalong was sailing. There was a dangerous sea storm. Many boats started to sink. Stormalong grabbed the boats. He put them on *The Courser*. He brought them to safety. He was fixing his sails. A big wind came. It threw Stormalong and his ship into the sky.

Stormalong was buried at sea.

DID YOU KNOW?

➤ People in Mississippi tell tall tales. They refer to it as "calling the dog." This started when a man hosted a contest. The contest awarded the biggest lie. Many people competed. They told tall tales. They wanted to win. The last contestant said, "I never told a lie in my life." He won a dog.

➤ In the early 1900s, people sent postcards. Postcards are cards with pictures. They're sent in the mail. There were special postcards. They were like tall tales. Photographers created tall tales with trick photography. They combined painting and photographs. They made people look bigger. They made people look like they were with monsters.

➤ A snipe hunt is a popular joke in North America. People tell tall tales about snipes. Snipes are described as furry bird-like animals that come out during full moons. People trick others into hunting for this creature.

CHALLENGE:

WRITE YOUR OWN TALE

> How tall will your tale be?

BEFORE YOU WRITE:
- Read more tall tales. Use them as models.
- Make a list of facts. Pick a fact. Turn it into a tall tale.
- Make a list of annoying things that happened to you. Think about ordinary problems. Use them to inspire story ideas.
- Read joke books. Learn how authors use humor.

AS YOU WRITE:
- Describe a problem.
- Create a silly solution to overcome the problem.
- Include a character that has heroic qualities or superpowers. Make sure the character has a goal.
- Include a setting in a local area.
- Include humor. Don't be afraid to write something really silly.
- Make sure to have exaggerated and realistic details. Exaggerated details provide humor. Realistic details let readers picture themselves in the story.
- Play with language. Use alliteration, like "The skinny seagull saw some sandwiches." Repeat words and phrases. Include rhyming words.
- Set up an ordinary sequence of events. Then, add a twist at the end. Surprise the reader by changing the story.

AFTER YOU WRITE:
- Proofread and edit your tall tale.
- Keep your tall tale brief. A good tall tale is about 3 to 5 minutes long.
- Practice reading your tall tale out loud. Film yourself.
- Host a "Tall Tales Contest." Invite people to share their tall tales. Give awards for the best tall tales.
- Host a "True Story or Tall Tale?" game. Have people share stories. Have audience members guess whether the story is true or a tall tale.

CONSIDER THIS!

TAKE A POSITION! Some people think tall tales are exaggerations of the truth. Other people think tall tales are lies. What do you think? Argue your point with reasons and evidence.

SAY WHAT? Today's tall tales are superhero stories. For example, compare Paul Bunyan and Superman. Explain how they're alike. Explain how they're different.

THINK ABOUT IT! Tall tales started in the 1800s. They started in the United States. Life wasn't easy for American settlers. Settlers are people who build towns. They worked hard all day. At night, they told stories around campfires. They bragged about their adventures. They competed with each other. These bragging contests became tall tales. What do you brag about? Do you exaggerate details? Why or why not?

LEARN MORE!

Myers, Christopher. *Lies and Other Tall Tales*. New York: Harper-Collins, 2005.

Osbourne, Mary Pope. *American Tall Tales*. New York: Knopf, 1991.

Powell, Martin. *Tall: Great American Folktales*. North Mankato, MN: Stone Arch Books, 2012.

GLOSSARY

beached (BEECHD) stuck or stranded on the beach

bragged (BRAGD) showed off

calamity (kuh-LAM-ih-tee) disaster, tragedy, big mess

exaggerate (ig-ZAJ-uh-rate) to stretch the truth in order to make things seem bigger than they are

funeral (FYOO-nur-uhl) a ceremony that honors a person's death

heroine (HER-oh-in) a female hero

lumberjack (LUHM-bur-jak) logger; worker who cuts down trees to make logs, which are used to make houses or buildings

masts (MASTS) tall poles on a ship used to hold sails

orphan (OR-fun) a child whose parents died

plains (PLAYNZ) flat lands

reins (RAYNZ) ropes used to control horses

smallpox (SMAWL-pahks) a deadly disease

stagecoach (STAYJ-kohch) a four-wheeled carriage pulled by horses used to transport people and things

whirlpool (WURL-pool) a rotating mass of water that sucks things in

INDEX

A
African Americans, 18–23

B
Babe the Blue Ox, 8–10
bragging, 4, 13 20
Bunyan, Paul, 6–11

C
Calamity Jane, 12–17
"calling the dog," 29
Cannary, Martha Jane. See Calamity Jane
Captain Stormalong, 24–28
Courser, The, 25–28

D
Deadwood, SD, 12, 16

G
giant, 6, 9, 10, 20, 24–28

H
hammer, 18, 21–22
Hausa people, 20
Henry, John, 18–23

K
kraken, 26

L
lies, 9, 29
lumberjacks, 10

M
Manly Man, 20
martial arts, 15
Mississippi, 29

N
Native Americans, 13, 15–16
Nigeria, 20
Norris, Chuck, 15

O
ox, 9–10

P
postcards, 29

R
railroads, 18–22

S
snipes, 29
Stormalong, Alfred Bulltop. See Captain Stormalong

W
Wild West, 12–17
women, 12–17